.50

THE
Old Photographs
SERIES
AROUND
CHEADLE

West end of High Street, Cheadle pre 1903. We see a relaxed street scene, showing a delivery boy, a horse drawn wagon and five of the many public houses in Cheadle at that time.

THE
Old Photographs
SERIES
AROUND
CHEADLE

Compiled by
W. George Short

CHALFORD

BATH • AUGUSTA • RENNES

First published 1994
Copyright © W. George Short, 1994

The Chalford Publishing Company Limited
St Mary's Mill, Chalford, Stroud
Gloucestershire GL6 8NX

ISBN 0 7524 0022 3

Typesetting & origination by
Alan Sutton Limited
Printed in Great Britain by
Redwood Books, Trowbridge

The young generation of Cheadle on the sports field, Mackenzie Senior School, Cheadle in 1958. Many of these young people will now have young families of their own. This book is dedicated to all those successive generations.

Contents

Looking east along High Street around 1909. This photograph was on a postcard sent by a nephew to a Mr A. Spooner, his uncle, who lived near to Liverpool. However, the postcard was sent back to Cheadle early in 1994 by a lady living in Natal, South Africa.

Introduction

Documentary evidence for the Cheadle area spans some nine centuries, but photographic evidence, on which this book concentrates, covers just over one hundred years.

This compilation of photographs first looks at our schooldays and activities connected with the churches and other organisations which formed a large part of the social life of the area.

We take a tour around the villages, where we see many fine buildings, regrettably some of which are no longer there. We look at all aspects of village life, including social and work related activities.

The area has seen many changes over the years. At the beginning of this century there were coal mines and silk and tape factories that employed many hundreds of workers. However, owing to changing demands, these industries have now gone and we look here at these and other aspects of working life that are no longer with us.

In days gone by many organisations, societies and choirs held processions and carnivals as a way of recruiting new members, getting the community involved and, perhaps, showing them the benefits of a socially enhanced life. Such displays were always very popular and would draw large crowds of people. Mass entertainments such as we know today were not available and community events were an important part of everyone's calendar. The fifth section of this book looks at those events in photographs.

Finally, we take a tour around Cheadle itself, showing scenes spanning the last hundred years. There are scenes here which have seen few changes and others which have changed beyond all recognition.

In compiling the photographs for this book, I have been keen to give local people as prominent a part as the town's buildings. It is the people who have formed the history which now unfolds.

I hope that this book will open the eyes of younger readers to the town they never knew and evoke happy memories of past times for the not so young.

W. George Short
Cheadle

One
Schools and Churches

The infants class of the Cheadle National Primary School around 1919, staging a 'wedding'. Miss Hannah Pyatt was the headmistress of the school at the time.

'Supporting the Suffragette Movement' at the Cheadle National Boys School around 1917.

A tableau at the Junior Girls' Church School in the 1920's.

Boys of the Cheadle Church School giving a physical education display in the 1920's. The old Cheadle hospital can be seen in the background.

A 'Band of Hope' tea party on the Rectory lawn in June 1892.

Centenary celebrations of St Giles Parish Church, Cheadle on 10th June 1939, showing the presentation of centenary purses. Featured in the photograph are Revd G.R. Thornton (centre), Sir Joseph Lamb MP and Bishop E.S. Woods, the Bishop of Lichfield.

Less formal centenary celebrations on the same day, a football match between the 'Mothers' and the Girls Friendly Society. The start was scheduled for 5.00pm with Mrs M.E. Blizzard to kick-off.

The kick-off, showing left to right; Miss Barrett, Mrs Crook, Mrs Phyllis Stevenson and Mrs Blizzard. The final score is, unfortunately, not known!

Cheadle Boys Church School c.1925, showing the headmaster Mr George Johnson. Mr Johnson was headmaster from 1924 to 1930.

Cheadle Girls Church School in November 1927. The headmistress at this time (not shown) was Mrs Fanny H. Coxon.

A tea party held in the Town Hall, Cheadle around 1910. The town hall later became the Osborne cinema, a bingo hall and then a night club, but now, sadly, it is empty. The gentlemen at the rear are, left to right, Mr C.J. Blagg (with beard), Mr Lowndes, Mr Malkin and Mr Steele.

A sewing class at St Michael's Mission Church, Ashbourne Road, c. 1910, with Revd E.S. Carlos, Rector of Cheadle on the right of the photograph. The ladies made hassocks and other articles for the church.

15

Cheadle Mother's Union, presenting a production of the pantomime Aladdin. The players featured are, left to right, Mrs J. Barker, Mrs M. Slack, Mrs M. Hurst, Mrs Archer, Mrs M. Booth, Mrs Thompson and Mrs Ainsworth and Mrs M. Collier on the right. The player who is third from the right has not been identified.

A church social event in the Carlos Institute in the 1950's.

Consecration of the churchyard extension at St Gile's Parish Church in 1963, with Revd S.E. Moore, the rector, Mr R. Collier and Mr R. Heath, the church wardens, Right Revd R.J. Clitheroe MA, Bishop of Stafford, the assistant registrar to the diocese and representing the parish council, Mr Brunt, Mr Hurst and Mr Beardmore.

Cheadle Wesleyan Church in Chapel Street. This was built in 1812 and demolished in 1966 to make way for the new building.

Ladies of the 'Bright Hour' at the Wesleyan Chapel, Cheadle around 1925.

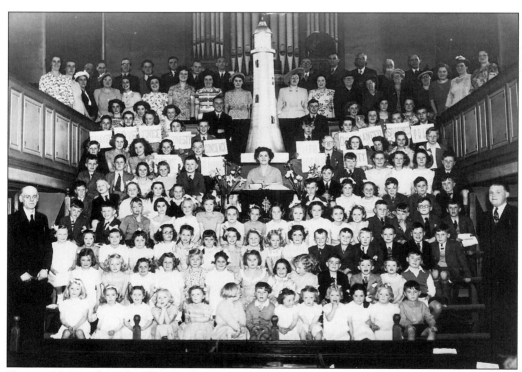

'Sitting Up' at the Cheadle Wesleyan Sunday School, depicting the 'Lighthouse', on Whit Sunday, 28th May 1950. 'Sitting Up' was a traditional celebration of the Sunday School anniversary. The conductors are Mr Arthur Keeling and Mr George Kinder.

Christmas 1949

The Nativity tableau at the Cheadle Wesleyan Church in 1949.

Teachers at the Cheadle Wesleyan Sunday School c. 1920.

Clergy and officials attending the Charles Street Methodist Church Centenary on 10th April 1948. The clergy shown are, left to right, Revd F.W. Henshall, Revd A. Jones, the rector of Cheadle, Revd F.H. Cumbers (standing), Revd J.H. Clucas, Revd W. Russell Shearer, Revd O.J. Beard and Revd J. Rogan.

Dr E. Mackenzie MD, governor of schools, Mr Barton Land, the headmaster of the County Primary School and Mr Birks, the headmaster of Cheadle Secondary School at a school function in the 1930's.

A Christmas party at the County Primary School in 1972. Mrs Perry was the teacher of this class, but Father Christmas was Mr Jack Ladkin.

Revd Walter Morris, seated at the front, who served the parish as priest of St Giles Roman Catholic Church for over sixty years, Revd Myscough, the curate and ladies of the Roman Catholic Church of Cheadle.

Bishop Griffin, later Cardinal Griffin, blessing two new bells at St Giles Roman Catholic Church in May 1939, assisted by Revd J.J. Macdonald. One bell was dedicated to the Sacred Heart and the other to Saint Joseph.

Two

Activities and Organisations

Prince George, Duke of Kent, passes Mr Ned Plant, Mr A.C. Holbrook, the workhouse master, and Mr Wetwood on his way to open the Monkhouse Community Centre in Back Street on 13th July 1934. Back Street was renamed Prince George Street to commemorate this visit.

Dr E. Mackenzie opens the Cheadle tennis courts in Lid Lane, Cheadle in 1932.

Cheadle Tennis Club, Lid Lane in 1939. Back row, left to right: N. Maclean, R. Fearns, - ? -. Middle row: F. Street, - ? -, Mrs Street, - ? -, C. Horton, Miss M. Lee, Miss J. Warren, J. Goodwin, - ? -. Front row: Miss H. Edwards, Miss Macarthy, Miss W. Marsden, Miss T. Spearing, Miss Garner, Miss H. Ratcliffe, Miss G. Williams and Miss D. Maclean.

A Cheadle Methodist United Guild tennis party at the Recreation Ground tennis courts in 1949.

Cheadle Girl Guide officers at the Candy Fair in 1939, showing, from left to right, the standard bearer, then, Miss Jean Phillips the Brown Owl, Mrs Berry, Mrs A. Philips, Mrs M. Bolton the District Commissioner, Miss Cornes and Miss Berry.

Cheadle Girl Guide and Brownies troops in 1939. Seated on the second row from the back are Miss J. Warren the Guide Captain, Mrs Bolton the District Commissioner and Miss J. Phillips the Brown Owl.

Girls Training Corps No.737 Company, Cheadle, in September 1942. Mrs Turner, the Corps Commander, is leading, followed by Miss Primrose Calland.

Cheadle Girl Guides in the Armistice Day Parade in Tean Road, Cheadle in 1946.

The 1st Cheadle Scouts Troop c. 1934, pictured in the garden behind the studio of Mr Lowndes in the High Street. Mr F. Shaw, the assistant Scout Master and Revd Thompson, the Scout Master are on the middle row.

The 1st Cheadle Cub Pack at the Scout Hut in the grounds of the Rectory in 1957. Miss Bond and Mrs Thompson, the assistants, the Cub Master Eric Titterton and his assistant Bob Walker are on the back row.

Members of the Cheadle Home Guard around 1942, pictured with their Spigot mortar gun. Back row, left to right: P. Wood, H. Smith, A. Billings, T. Burnett and T. Timmis. Front row: R. Botham, J. Mason, J. Brunt and D. Spooner.

Cheadle Home Guard at camp at Wetton Mill in the Manifold Valley, showing J. Mason, E. Millward, F. Brunt and Mr Wetwood.

Cheadle ARP wardens, 1941 to 1945. Back row, left to right: C. Marshall, R. Shaw, - ? -, V. Pepper, B. Wright and B. Keates. Front row: F. Jones, J. Beech, W. Brown, -? -.

The ARP post situated at the Hilton Gravel Works at Mobberley with, from left to right: B. Wright, W. Brown, F. Jones and V. Pepper.

Mr Alfred Hurst invites Mrs L. Holmes to unveil a clock presented to the Cheadle Bowling Club in the memory of her late husband, Len, on 25th May 1962.

Mrs Holmes, members and spectators at Cheadle Bowling Club under the clock, now unveiled.

Members of Cheadle Bowling Club in the 1920's, Mr Mosely, William Ball, Dr E. Mackenzie and Bob Woodward.

Cheadle Liberal Club billiards team in the 1920's.

The Cheadle Hiker's Club pictured in June 1927 outside the Town Hall, Cheadle, at the start of a walk to Ilam. Pictured, left to right, are B. Barker, K. Green, D. Green, E. Harrison, N. Worsley, D. Plant, J.A. Alcock, J.P. Keates, J. Worsley, Mr Marland and H. Hurst.

By the banks of the Cheadle Swimming Pool at Litley Farm c. 1902. The pool was controlled by the parish council from July 1902 until March 1908.

Red Cross workers at St Giles House, Cheadle in 1941. They were responsible, amongst other things, for making equipment, sewing and knitting.

Cheadle Choral Society in 1941. The photograph was taken on the occasion of the conductor, Mr Fenna (centre of the second row), leaving to join the services in the Second World War.

The Golden Jubilee celebrations of Queen Victoria on 21st June 1887. The Cheadle Fire Brigade are seen in the procession, being preceded by the Cheadle Brass Band. The banner and members of the 'Oddfellows' can be seen on the left.

Denstone College was partly destroyed by fire on 25th May 1894. It is recorded that 'Cheadle Fire Brigade was first to get their engine to work and throw water on the burning buildings'. The roof at the centre and right of the main building was destroyed.

The naming ceremony of the new motor fire engine, called Victor, on 17th December 1931. Pictured in the photograph, from the left are, Fire Captain F. Cox, Revd Bedson and G.V. Phillips.

Mr G.V. Phillips attends his last meeting as chairman of the Cheadle Fire Brigade on 12th July 1940. Mr Phillips is pictured at the centre of the front row with second officer Ned Plant to the left and chief officer, C.W. Lawrence and third officer, E. Durose, to the right.

A fire at Sheppey's Fish and Chip shop in High Street, Cheadle on 20th March 1953.

Messengers of the Cheadle Fire Brigade at the fire station in Tean Road during the Second World War. Back row, left to right: F. Martin, K. Wright, R. Lucas, C. Pargeter, W. Wetwood, B. Lovatt, B. Snow, A. Allen and G.V. Bracking, the divisional officer..Front row: A. Hill, G. Allen, C. Wood and E. Woodward.

Cheadle Militia are given a meal at Cheadle railway station, prior to their journey to Lichfield Barracks, August 1914.

The Parish Council and Inhabitants of Cheadle

request the honour of your company at a

Knife and Fork Tea and Smoking Concert

On Wednesday, 30th July, at 5 o'clock, 1919

At the Town Hall, Cheadle.

E. Mackenzie, Chairman.

F. Holmes, Clerk.

If you accept the invitation please give in your name at once to Mr. F. HOLMES, at the Parish Office, Cheadle ; or Mr. J. COOLING, Secretary of the Comrades of the Great War Association ; or Mr. B. WOOD, at the Town Hall, Cheadle.

LOWNDES, PRINTER, CHEADLE.

An invitation from the parish council to all inhabitants and former Great War servicemen to a concert. 'The Comrades of the Great War Association' referred to in the invitation was a forerunner of the British Legion.

The unveiling of the war memorial panels by Lord Dartmouth at the Recreation Ground, Tean Road on 3rd September 1923.

Cheadle Memorial Recreation Ground, Tean Road. The memorial panels can be seen fixed to the gate pillars and the memorial plinth inside the gates. The panels were not fixed to the plinth, as originally intended, as the gun mounted on top of it was of German origin.

Members of the Cheadle British Legion pose for a photograph prior to boarding a special train taking them to a British Legion rally in 1937. The rally included an inspection by HM King George VI and Queen Elizabeth.

Drumhead service at High Shutt, held by members of the area branches of the British Legion on Sunday 25th July 1937. The service was conducted by the Rector of Checkley, Revd E. Drinkwater.

The Cheadle branch of the Royal British Legion, Women's Section, in an Armistice Day Parade in the 1970's.

The Earl of Shrewsbury unlocks the door at the opening of the Ex-Service Centre in Bank Street, Cheadle on 2nd November 1946, supported by Mr W. Shaw, secretary, Dr Coullie, president and Mr H. Perkin, chairman of the Cheadle British Legion.

The 'Wings for Victory' parade at Tean Road Recreation Ground in 1944.

The Cheadle branch of the Royal British Legion, Men's Section, saluting Dr E. Evison, the chairman, during an Armistice Day Parade in the 1950's.

The National Union of General Workers, 50th anniversary float at a Cheadle Carnival in the 1930's. Pictured left to right are F. Hudson, J. Hall, F. Rowley, J. Mason, - ? -, G. James, J. Ainsworth and J. Poole.

Cheadle Masonic Lodge (No. 1587). The picture, taken in the 1930's, shows Mr A.C. Holbrook, the workhouse master, as the Worshipful Master. The first meeting of the Cheadle lodge took place on 17th May 1876.

The 1st Cadet Division of St. John's Ambulance Brigade. When it started in the 1950's, eighty two girls applied to join and fifty six of these cadets qualified in 1952. Dr Richards, the County Commissioner from Stafford, can be seen on the back row, third from the right.

Mrs F.M. Willis receives her order of 'Serving Sister' in the St. John's Ambulance Brigade at an investiture ceremony held at the St. John's headquarters, London on 22nd July 1969. Mrs Willis and Mrs E. Cox are the only two Serving Sisters in Cheadle.

Mr E. Spooner being invested with the order of 'Serving Brother' in October 1973.

Winners of the St. Joh's Ambulance Brigade 'Oliver Shield' first aid competition in 1936. Pictured, left to right, are E. Spooner, J. Swain and R. Rowley standing and E. Durose and R. Johnson, seated.

The first committee of the Cheadle Old Age Pensioners' Association in September 1949. Mr G.V. Bracking, seated in the centre, was appointed secretary, a post he still holds in 1994.

Mrs E. Fynney cuts the turf to signify the start of the building of the Cheadle Swimming Baths in July 1966. To Mrs Fynney's left is Mr T. Willis, the secretary of the Bath's Committee and to her right is Mr H. Cornes, the contractor. The swimming baths opened on 2nd September 1967.

Cheadle Senior School, the winners of the local schools football trophy in 1950, showing Mr H. Chester, the sports master on the left and Mr Gibbs, the headmaster on the right.

The RAF football XI 'C' team. During the 1942/43 season, this team won the Longton League Cup, the May Bank Cup, the final of which was played at Port Vale FC's ground and the Staffs Junior Cup, the final of which was played at Stoke City FC's ground.

Cheadle Cricket Club, 1st team in 1926. Back row, left to right: Mr Rowlands (umpire), S. Capewell, E. Critchlow, JP Keates, B. Brough, F. Boardman, V. Pepper, P. Ball (scorer), Mr Edmonds and Mr Hunt (umpire). Front row, left to right: B. Barker, J. Shaw, H.Capewell, R. Whitehurst, J. Whitehurst and C. Chandler.

Cheadle Church Boys' School, Inter School Trophy winners in 1934. Back row, left to right: M. James, W. Basnett, F. Millward, P.S. Thorley, H. Capewell and G. Durose. Middle row: Master Carr, B. Smith, A. Broatch, V. Woodward, Dr E. Mackenzie, S. Whitehurst and R. Rushton. Front row: A. Wright, D. Lees, B. Sleigh, J. Mason, J. Sales, A. Morris.

The opening ceremony of the new Cheadle Rural District Council Offices on 5th March 1937. Pictured, left to right, are W. Podmore, F.S. Cox, clerk, Alderman J.A. Dale the Lord Mayor of Stoke on Trent, D. Heath JP the chairman of Cheadle Rural District Council and J.H. Aberley, the vice chairman.

Council members and friends pictured on the dissolution of Cheadle Rural District Council on 29th March 1974. The last chairman, pictured in the centre, was Mr J.E. Brassington. Mrs Tunstall, third person from the left on the front row, was the last chairman of Cheadle Parish Council and the first mayor of Cheadle.

Three
Around the Villages

Blythe Bridge railway station, opened on 7th August 1848. The gates shown in the photograph were replaced by a barrier in March 1980.

Cresswell railway station in 1952. The station was demolished in the 1960's and the signal box on the right was demolished on 19th February 1989. Both Blythe Bridge and Cresswell are on the Stoke to Derby line.

The Bulls Head public house in Forsbrook c. 1900. The licensees were Mr and Mrs Heath. This public house was demolished in the 1950's.

Dairy Farm, known as 'Blake Hall' on Delphouse Bank, just outside Cheadle. The house had a sitting room, kitchen, five large bedrooms and 137 acres of land when it was sold in 1943 for £2,675.

The Elms, also on Delphouse Bank, a nineteenth-century house with fourteen acres of land, which was sold in 1943 for £1,475.

The junction of New Road and High Street, Tean, with a stagecoach passing along a street decorated for a celebration, perhaps a jubilee or a coronation.

Postman Ferneyhough on his delivery round in Normacott Road, Tean c. 1910.

Ex-servicemen on inspection at Oakhill, Tean prior to a 'Jubilee Supper' on 16th May 1935.

A rear view of 'The Heybridge', Lower Tean. This house was built in 1813 as a family home of one branch of the Philips family and it was demolished in the 1950's.

The Dog and Partridge public house, Lower Tean in the 1930's.

Members of the Junior Red Cross groups from Tean and Freehay and the St. John's Ambulance Brigade, Alton at a rally held at Heath House, Tean in the 1930's. Heath House is still a family home of the Philips family.

A rear view of the Double Row, Tean. These eight houses were built in 1798, with workers living downstairs and looms situated upstairs. In 1822 the looms were resited in the mill and the houses were converted fully into living accommodation. They were finally demolished in 1966.

Revd R.W. Hubball, Revd D.W. Watson and Revd C.E. Collin pictured after conducting the closing service at the Methodist United Church, Tean on 29th December 1985.

'The Temple', Tean. The columns were part of Heath House from 1690 until 1836, then in 1837 they were erected in the woods by the Hollington Road outside Tean, now known as Temple Wood.

Rt Revd R.J. Clitheroe MA the Bishop of Stafford conducts a confirmation service at Christ Church, Tean, assisted by the vicar, Revd John Dodd in 1963.

High Street, Tean in the 1930's. The shoe shop on the left was run by Ted and Hilda Moult and it was demolished in 1954.

The 'Rocks' at Huntley. The road was cut through in 1818 to conform with the Turnpike Act.

St Chad's Church, Freehay, built to the design of Messrs Scott and Moffat in 1843 and consecrated in 1846.

Plantation House and Farm, near to Freehay, built in 1855 for Thomas Mackenzie. When the family left, the house was used as a vicarage to St Chad's Church, Freehay until 1927. It is now a private residence.

Woodhead Hall near Cheadle. It was built in 1873, by Sugden of Leek, for the Shepherd Allen family. The hall has twenty eight rooms and is now owned by the Crown.

The interior of Woodhead Hall. This photograph was taken between 1925 and 1936, when the hall was being used as a preparatory school.

Laying one of the foundation stones of the Kingsley Holt Methodist Church on 24th July 1937. The minister on the right is Revd Henshall.

St Werburgh's Church, Kingsley. The picture shows the original tower which dates from 1221 and the nave which was rebuilt in 1819.

The Shawe, Kingsley c. 1908. Formerly the home of the Stubbs and Beech families, it was rebuilt in 1821 but it was demolished in 1987.

The building of St Mildred's Church, Whiston around 1910. The picture, taken at the old copper mills, shows workers and teams moving some 500 tons of stone to the church site. The local farmers lent the horses and carts and the work was done on a voluntary basis in holidays and spare time.

The opening ceremony of the Hawksmoor Nature Reserve, owned by the National Trust, on 7th May 1927. The leading gentleman, with papers in hand, is Mr J.R.B. Masefield, with Lord Grey and Lord Dartmouth following.

Opening day at the Hawksmoor Nature Reserve, showing (see small numbers above heads) 1, Captain Unwin VC, 2, Lord Stafford, 3, Lord Grey, 4, Lord Dartmouth, 5, Lady Farmer and 9, Joseph Quinton Lamb MP.

The Gatehouse, Oakamoor around 1920. Mr Peter Birks was the gatehouse keeper. This building and the tunnel entrance to the left can still be found near to the public picnic area.

The busy railway in Oakamoor in the 1920's, transporting goods from Bolton's Brass and Copper Works, later to be resited at Froghall, as well as taking passengers to Leek and Uttoxeter.

Oakamoor c. 1910, showing the Cricketer's Arms public house and, to the right, the old toll-gate house.

Oakamoor tennis courts in 1893. Houses were built on the site in 1907 and it is now known as 'Tennis Corner'.

The unveiling of the Oakamoor War Memorial on 1st April 1922. The memorial was erected by Pattisons of Oakamoor.

Kerry's of Oakamoor acquired this Ford Laundlette van for deliveries in 1930.

Holy Trinity Church, Oakamoor was built in 1832 as a dual purpose building, the ground floor being used as a National School. Note the two doors at the eastern end for the school and that the church is all on the the first floor. The school was closed in 1859.

Farley Hall in Farley. The original hall was built around 1609, with extensive alterations being made in 1784. The large semi-circular glasshouse with a domed-roof was added in the mid-nineteenth century. The hall is now a private residence.

The limestone workings at Froghall. The large drum in the centre background controlled the movements of the trucks, which were joined by a cable, on an automatic pulley system. Full trucks coming downhill from Whiston and Cauldon hauled the empty ones back up the hill to be refilled.

Break time on Foxt bridge c. 1910. This charming photograph was taken by W.H. Nithsdale of Leek and is typical of the inimitable style of his pictures.

Froghall lime kilns in the 1920's. The works closed in 1944 and the site is now a public picnic area.

A tranquil scene at the Bolton's works at Froghall in the 1920's.

The 'lock up' at Alton. It was built in 1815 and renovated in 1977.

Alton Bridge, built in 1808/9 by Henry Fower at a cost of £502 2s 7d.

The banquet hall at Alton Towers designed by A.W.N. Pugin and built in 1845. The photograph was taken in the 1930's, when the hall was used as a Tea Room. The wood panelling was lost in the fire of 1948.

Visitors on a tour of the grounds at Alton Towers in the early part of this century. The grounds were first opened to the public in 1832.

Four
People at Work

The opening of the 'Klondyke' New Haden Colliery in 1907. At the time, the colliery was owned by the Bassono brothers and the manager was Mr Haines.

The Park Hall Colliery was opened in 1876 and this photograph shows the Rescue Squad No.1 c. 1914, comprising, left to right: Tom Brough of Kingsley, Jack Morton of Cellarhead, Jim Barnes who was later killed at New Haden Colliery, Mr Clifford the instructor based at Berry Hill pit, Bob Fisher, Fred Shaw of Harplow and Tom Twigg.

The site of Cheadle Park Colliery on Leek Road was prepared in 1884 and the first shaft was sunk in 1886. The first load of coal was raised on 17th June 1887 and it was taken to the owner, Mr A.S. Bolton at Moor Court. The colliery was closed in 1915.

A group of men and boys who worked at the Cheadle Park Colliery for half a day on 16th December 1899 for the Boer War Fund.

Laying charges to fell the 'Brassworks' chimney at Brookhouses on 8th June 1907. The photograph shows, left to right: Mr Tunnicliff (son), Mr Tunnicliff (father), Mr Bolton, G. Beardmore, Miss Eve Beardmore, later Mrs Lovatt, A. Shenton and Miss Elsie Beardmore, later Mrs Alcock.

The remains of the chimney after felling. When the 'Brassworks' were in operation from 1725 to 1835 there were nine 'sheds' and thirty six furnaces.

'Outcropping' along the Race Course Fields, Leek Road around 1926. There were two sizes of hole being operated, an eighteen yard hole and a ten yard hole, both four feet wide at the seam. The Number 9 hole pictured was operated by the Heathcote family.

Working at their hole at Race Course Fields, from the left, are: Mr Whitehurst, Fred Robinson, Jack Lovatt, - ? -, Jim Locker at the rear, George Shaw seated, Ern Wood and Fred Croft.

Mr Shaw in the pump room at the Cheadle Water Works. The steam engine pictured was dismantled in December 1934 and replaced by an oil-fired engine.

Joseph Hurst's Builders and Timber Shop, Bank Street, Cheadle in the 1930's, featuring, left to right: John Yates, Harold Bolton, Jim Hurst and other joiners.

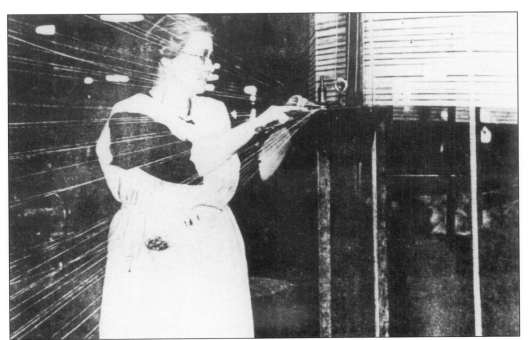

Mrs Monica Wilson operating the old type of hand driven warping machine. Mrs Wilson was employed at J. and N. Philips of Tean for over 47 years.

A fire at the Brough Nicholson and Hall Silk Mill in Oakamoor Road on 28th April 1952. The building was later demolished and a JCB factory now stands on the site.

Mary Ladkin and Barbara Beardmore operating Jacquard looms, which produced labels, at the Brough Nicholson and Hall Silk Mill in the autumn of 1952.

Vincent Chandler and Ken Crook putting up the blackout blinds at the Silk Mill in September 1939.

Jacquard and Silk loom maintenance crew in the 'new' shed at the Silk Mill in 1951.

Mr Jack Heath, the blacksmith, at his forge in Queen Street. He traded as a blacksmith for over 70 years.

Fallow's Butchers at the corner of Cross Street, Cheadle. Miss Mary and Miss Elizabeth Fallows kept this business from the early 1900's until the 1930's and then it was taken over by Mr Robert Salt. The premises are now occupied by Staffordshire Building Society.

Miss M. Underhill and Mrs F. Moss in the grocery section of George Moss's shop in Cross Street in the 1950's. Note the old bacon slicer and the Easter Eggs.

Miss Annie Pyatt, greengrocer of Back Street, now Prince George Street. Miss Pyatt sold her produce around the area going as far as Oakamoor, Alton and Kingsley during the 1920's and 1930's.

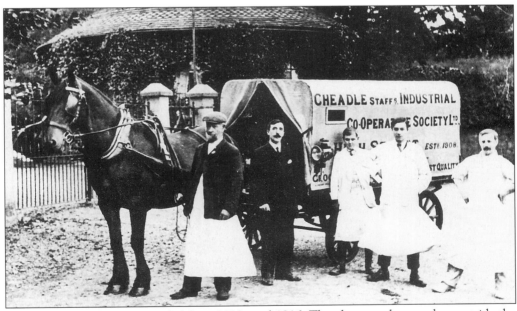

Cheadle Industrial Co-op, traded from 1908 until 1916. The photograph was taken outside the Round House, Back Street c. 1915 and it features, left to right: Thomas Hill, Mr Crowther, Bart Massey, Charlie Phillips and Mr Marsh.

John Morton, groom and coachman to the Blagg family, with Miss Dorothy's horse 'Daphne' at Green Hill House, now demolished, c. 1890.

For hundreds of years farming has been one of the Cheadle area's main sources of employment. Here we see a 1880/90 reaper machine used for cutting grass or corn. This machine was to be replaced some years later by a sail reaper machine.

Mrs Shaw of Charles Street, c. 1930, doing the family wash using a 'dolly peg and tub', the forerunner of today's washing machines!

Mr Bramwell Shaw with some of his hens around 1980. Mr Shaw was a coal merchant for many years, using a horse and cart for his deliveries, but he gave this up in the 1950's to concentrate on farming. The photograph shows the former engine house of the Malkin's pit, built in 1876, which was on Mr Shaw's land.

Mr Bernard Harrison delivering oil to customers living in caravans on Cheadle Park in the 1950's. Bernard was often seen around Cheadle pushing an old pram full of oil cans.

Plants' lorries waiting to be loaded with sand and other aggregates to be taken to Liverpool, at the Hilton Gravel Works, Mobberley, in the 1960's.

A lorry belonging to J.A. Baileys takes away the market cross in High Street, Cheadle on 24th July 1980 for renovation work. The cross was returned a week later.

Mr Shaw, gunsmith and lockmaker of Back Street, Cheadle in the 1890's.

Five

Processions, Carnivals and Gatherings

The Ancient Order of Forresters, in their costumes used for walks which usually took place on Whit Monday. This photograph was taken in the yard of the Unicorn public house around 1910.

The 'Crown Jewels' float in a procession through Cheadle High Street, presented by the Cheadle (Church of England) Girls School, c. 1925. Mr Bob Plant is pictured leading the horse.

Doug Lees and Cyril Smith with the New Zealand Lamb Carnival Bicycle owned by Mr G.W. Lees, in the 1930's.

The King and Queen of the Carnival being presented to Dr George Saint and his wife on the Greyhound Field in 1926. The Carnival 'Folly' on the left of the picture, Miss Edith Spooner, is wearing a dress made of red and white crepe paper.

Maypole dancing on the Greyhound Field c. 1925.

Sunday schools and church organisations assemble in the Market Square in the 1930's.

A presentation to Sergeant Chandler from the Town on being awarded the Distinguished Conduct Medal on 18 February 1918.

The 1st Cheadle Cubs in an Armistice Day Parade, led by the Cub Master, Eric Titterton, in 1967.

Members of the Order of Oddfellows in a procession along Cheadle High Street in the 1920's.

The League of Nations Union floats in a Cheadle Carnival. The league was formed in 1920, with 42 countries being represented and it held its final meeting in April 1946, when its functions were taken over by the United Nations Organisation.

A Corpus Christi procession passing the Market Square.

Choir and clergy in a Corpus Christi procession in 1934.

Cheadle miners waiting to go into the bank to draw unemployment pay during the strikes of 1928/29.

Collection of horses on 10th August 1914. The horses were medically examined by Mr Cope in the Wheatsheaf yard before being taken to Lichfield for service with the army.

St Giles' Parish Church choir leading a procession along High Street. On the right of the clergy is Revd Hon Weld Forrester, Rector of Cheadle from 1929 to 1936.

St Giles Parish Church choir and sunday school return to church after the procession.

The Pierrot's and Britannia floats at Cheadle Carnival c. 1922.

A 'Ride a Cock Horse' float presented by the infants class of the Cheadle Church school c. 1930. One of the two lorries owned by Cheadle Rural District Council at that time can be seen on the left.

Mr Jim Taylor's public address system on his 1947 Humber Buick.

'Those were the days' entry for the Cheadle Carnival in 1950. The stage coach was loaned by Mr Aubrey Lymer of Tean and the horses were loaned by Mr Poultney.

'Beside the seaside' float, entered by Brough Nicholson and Hall in the 1950 Carnival.

Mr and Mrs Jack Ratcliffe opening a Cheadle Old Age Pensioners' bazaar, along with Mr Wetwood, Mrs Whieldon, Mr Lovatt and the secretary, Mr G.V. Bracking.

Waiting for a procession on the 'Terrace Steps'. The steps were taken down some years ago as they were considered to be a road hazard.

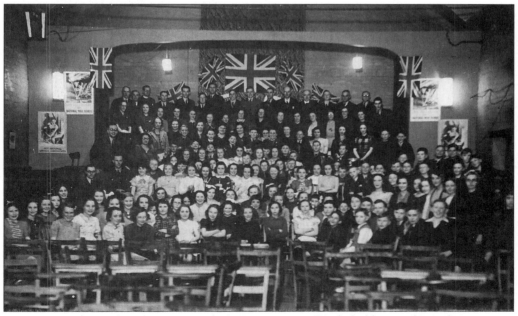

A concert in the Carlos Institute in aid of War Weapons Week, held on 2nd March 1941.

The Cheadle Subscription Band at The Elms in 1921.

Slaters' New Haden Band. Mr Slater donated the silver instruments to thank the workers for the production of one thousand tons of coal per week for three consecutive weeks at the New Haden Colliery.

The New Melody Dance Band comprising, left to right: Sam Walker, Aubrey Bentley, Arthur Parker, Bill Lund, Bill Mason, Eric Plant and Alf Malkin. The black drapes were used as a mark of respect for Bill Yates, a former member who was killed in Egypt in 1942.

The Pioneers Dance Band, who played in and around Cheadle from 1945 to 1955. Left to right: Alan Sargeant, Sam West, Alf Malkin, Bill Harris, Ralph Shaw and Dorothy Shaw.

RAF Cheadle 'Skyriders Dance Orchestra', who played between 1940 and 1945, pictured in the Guild Hall, Cheadle. On the right is Ken Jones, the conductor and on the left is M. Macdonald, the vocalist.

Church Lads' Brigade Cheadle No. 1 Squad around 1906. Back row, left to right: Mr Hudson the captain, James Mason, William Phillip Keates, William James and Harold Kirkham. Seated: Daniel Dearden and James Nixon, who was boys' teacher at the National School.

The Kingsley Band around 1910.

The Oakamoor Brass Band, led by Harry Collier, c. 1913.

Dr Mackenzie on the slide at the opening of the playing area on the Cheadle Recreation Ground, Tean Road in 1934.

Dr Mackenzie presenting a rocking horse at Cheadle Recreation Ground in celebration of the Silver Jubilee of King George V on 6th May 1935.

Six
Cheadle Scenes

Cheadle Toll House at the corner of Froghall Road and Leek Road. The house was built in 1835 and demolished in March 1963.

A Cheadle scene from around eighty years ago, showing the Town Hall which was built in 1894.

A view from near to the Town Hall, showing The Black Horse Inn on the right and The Black Horse Stables on the left. Mr Arthur Rushton was the last person to live in the accommodation available above the stables, c. 1905. Beyond the stables, The Alton Castle Inn can be seen.

Carriages returning from church after the wedding of Miss Blagg in 1885. The street decorations had been erected in honour of the wedding.

The east end of High Street in 1885, with Keates Furniture Warehouse on the left. Mr Keates, who was also the undertaker, can be seen standing in the road with his son in shirt sleeves. Further along the road there is a gap in the buildings. The three shops that now stand on that site were built in 1899.

Mr William Cope outside his butchers shop in 1913, with his prize winning carcasses.

Mr Ralph Alcock's Furniture Warehouse in High Street. The building dates back to the 1820's and the Alcock family continued there in business until the 1960's. The building now houses a Superdrug store.

The District Bank premises in High Street, prior to demolition in 1976.

At 8.25 am on Sunday 31st October 1976 demolition work started on the District Bank building. By the end of the day, the premises were completely demolished.

HIGH STREET. CHEADLE.

Looking east along High Street in 1900. On the left side was a private residence of the Godwin family, Harvey's Drapers and Hilton's Boot and Shoe Makers and on the right side was Marshall's Chemists, Shenton's Printers and Stationers, Keates' Tearooms and Heath's butchers.

Looking west along High Street in 1885. The Market Cross is decorated in honour of Miss Blagg's wedding.

The Wheatsheaf Inn on the left and Hilton's Booterie at the top of Cross Street.

Mr Hellin, the then manager of Hilton's Booterie, won a Christmas shop window decoration competition in the early 1920's with this display.

The Market Cross, Cheadle c. 1904. Early records show that Cheadle was granted a Buttery Cross Order in 1652 and the cross would have marked the limit of Market Street, which later became High Street. To the left of the cross, on the way down Cross Street, Elliott's Linen and Drapers shop can be seen and on the right there is Fallows the butchers and Wm Shufflebotham & Sons, the plumbers.

Barclays Bank Limited at 62, High Street, prior to its closure in 1924. A bank had been on this site since 1877, first the Midland Banking Co, which was then absorbed into the Birmingham, Dudley & District Banking Co in 1881. In 1882, Cheadle is mentioned as one of this bank's thirty three branches. In 1912, this bank merged with the United Counties Bank, which in turn became Barclay & Co Limited on 1st January 1916. This building later became Wyles shoe shop and it is now Evan's jewellers.

Looking west along High Street in the 1970's. From left to right, there is Kemps the chemists, Albert Pepper's Stationers and agent for the Halifax Building Society, Hood's Fish and Chip Shop and further along is The Royal Oak Hotel.

Looking east along High Street c. 1908. The Tudor houses on the right had only recently had a plaster facade removed to expose the beams which can still be seen today.

The north side of High Street, showing the Old Royal Oak, open between 1818 and 1908 and Jackson's, Ironmonger, Nailmaker and agricultural implement maker. Over the period from 1818 to 1988 a series of ironmongers operated from this site, first Marson's, then Johnson's, Bagshaw's, Jackson's, Wasburn's and now Chester's.

The greengrocer's shop of John and Kate Pyatt at the corner of Church Street and High Street c. 1910.

Looking along Church Terrace, with the Church gate just visible on the right. The gate was taken away during the Second World War for munitions. Revd Carlos can be seen crossing the road near to the fountain, erected in 1879, on his way from the building which served as the Rectory from 1758 to 1982. This building is now The Manor Guest House.

Approaching Cheadle from the west c. 1915. On the left is the Portabello Inn, open from 1818 to 1922 and the former Police Station, from 1847 to 1915, which is now the St Giles Masonic Lodge.

The old Talbot Inn, first recorded in 1784. To the right of the picture the stables, which were converted into the Palace Cinema in 1914, can be seen. The old Talbot Inn was demolished in 1926.

The new Talbot Inn, built by Heaths of Tunstall in 1926 and opened in 1927. The building to the right had by this stage been converted into a cinema which was demolished in 1962.

Mr J.C. Keates, Mr Alfred Waugh and Mr Tipper pictured standing outside Mr Waugh's house in Watt Place, which also served as his stonemasons premises, c. 1905.

Construction of the Cheadle Senior School in The Avenue in 1930. J. Hurst of Cheadle was awarded the contract to build the school at a cost of £15,489. The heating contract was awarded to Truswells of Newcastle at a figure of £790.

Charles Street at the turn of the century.

Mrs Swetnam, with her son-in-law Will Pyatt, outside her shop at the corner of Charles Street and New Street, now Tape Street, around 1910.

The Mansion, Cheadle, which was built in 1869. Mr Harry Chadwick can be seen holding the reins of the carriage on the left. Mr E. Barker and Mr Thomas Plant are standing between the carriages and Mr Plant's sons, William and Thomas, are on the carriage on the right. The Mansion was demolished in 1978 and senior citizens' bungalows now stand on the site which is named Mansion Close.

Mr Bob Harris, newsagent in Ashbourne Road, Cheadle, in the early 1920's. He held the contract for the delivery of all Sunday newspapers until 1964, when the contract was sold to Porter's newsagents and grocers in Ashbourne Road.

Mr Sidney Plant, Mrs Mary Plant, Miss Dora Plant and Mr Jim Plant outside the public house called The Rifleman's Arms c. 1920, which stood at the corner of Chapel Street and Tape Street. It was demolished in July 1989.

Cheadle Textiles, formerly J. & N. Philip's tape factory, which stood on this site from 1798. The factory was partly demolished in 1973 and the preserved part in the centre now houses the Kwik Save store.

Demolition of the tape mill chimney commences on 28th May 1973. The demolition work was carried out by Rafferty Brothers.

The Alton Castle Inn at the corner of Queen Street and Tape Street in the 1890's. Mr John Poultney was licensee at this time.

The tape mill houses in Queen Street, built for J. & N. Philips in 1868 to accommodate their workers transferred from Eagley in Lancashire. There is a number and the initials NP, standing for Nathaniel Philips, over the doorways.